Happy Birthday Aunty Emma!
   Hope you have a nice
day and a happy, happy year!
I hope we get to see eachother
one of these years! I miss you.
                    Happy Birthday,
Hi Uncle   Love Gwen
Gordon!!   xoxo

As we pass through lifes milestones, it is
comforting to reflect on the people we have known
who have influenced our lives + we theirs; on our
family + on our accomplishments - for we always have
a base to work from which provides a springboard
for our future activities through the coming years.
                    Happy "50th"
                         Brian

17 or 32 - Baseball

GIFTS OF AGE

〜〜〜〜〜

A BOOK OF DAYS

Text by Charlotte Painter

Photography by Pamela Valois

CHRONICLE BOOKS • SAN FRANCISCO

Printed in Japan.

ISBN 0-87701-599-6

Distributed in Canada by: Raincoast Books, 112 East Third Ave., Vancouver, B.C., V5T ITC

10 9 8 7 6 5 4 3 2 1

Design by Herman + Company

Chronicle Books
275 Fifth St.
San Francisco CA 94103

A Note from the Author

The lives of the women in this book are filled with rare imagery, some of it quite small in size but often shimmering with beauty. Virginia Woolf called such images "moments of being," when a shock causes the cotton wool of ordinary existence to fall away from reality itself, to reveal richness and meaning.

These women spoke about living as part of a cyclic process, and of death as part of the cycle of life. I found most of them fearless about death, although there was anxiety about the prospect of ill health and frailty. There was a strong desire to live as long as health and functioning last. They expressed enormous joie de vivre, interest, excitement, adventurousness, passion.

Many older women are becoming free to act independently for the first time in age. Previously held back by the demands of families and husband, they are at last able to discover who they really are, and to remember what as children and young women they liked to do or dreamed of doing.

They also became *more* of what they had always been, freer to express themselves. Pretenses dropped; white lies became unnecessary. The past became more present, and their backgrounds more deeply valued. All these women, whether Asian, Black, American Indian, Hispanic, or white, expressed a connection with their origins more passionate in age than ever before.

Common among all, too, was a sense of faith, in as many forms as there are individuals, from spiritualism to agnosticism. Although several expressed themselves as religious skeptics, they too are sustained by faith in life itself, in the young, in the human race, whatever its origins and destiny. Their practices, in crafts and arts, in human relations, in healing and meditation, reflect that faith. That quality above all others makes its appeal to those younger than they as a source of inspiration.

When I first looked at these photographs, I became aware of a fear of aging that had always been at the back of my mind. Writing about these women would be a way of advancing toward what I feared, always the better part of valor, I believed. But as I progressed, I didn't find an enemy and I began to see that my fears themselves were cotton wool. The reality behind the wrinkles of these women became visible as a series of small shocks, each with their moment of enlightenment.

The greying of America is an irreversible process, and as we grow used to looking at older people, we can find joy in it. These women can help us. They *live* in the moment, like true existentialists, released from the burden of the past and without fear of the future. Their faces are easy to look at, for they hold something that invites reflection. And in their hearts there is a lightness we might all emulate, and a grace.

Charlotte Painter, 1989

A Note from the Photographer

Several years ago I read an essay by Elizabeth Janeway, "Breaking the Age Barrier," in which she speaks of our need to overcome the stereotypes of aging, which are based on the sick and needy rather than on the healthy and fulfilled. At the time I knew one remarkable older woman, my photography teacher, Ruth Bernhard. She was in her late sixties, and a number of us met with her regularly each month for critiques. During this period, I realized I needed an experienced woman friend to help me understand the problems I would face in midlife—how to balance a career with my friendships and family and how to further my own personal development while being involved with motherhood. I found myself studying Ruth to see how she managed such things in her own life. In contrast to the stereotypes, she seemed to grow *more* vigorous each year into her seventies.

Then I got to know my landlady and neighbor, Jacomena Maybeck. My husband and I felt fortunate to be renting a house she owned, a magical, rambling cottage in the Berkeley hills. Shortly after moving in, I went out and found her, barefoot, dressed in a halter top and shorts, energetically sloshing tar over leaky spots on the roof of her house. She was seventy-eight at the time. I realized that no stereotype of older women could account for Jackie. We became great friends. My relationship with her is the inspiration for this book.

A widow, Jacomena has a career in ceramics and has introduced me to many active and interesting women in their seventies and eighties. I began to think about what these women meant to me and why I was so drawn to them. Their relationships with others appeared to me deeper, more enduring than those of younger people I knew. These older women have continued to change and develop. I found them democratic, spontaneous, open to new experiences.

As a photographer, I set out to build a collective portrait of these women. I hoped that some of their character might come through in their postures, their gestures, their faces and expressions. I asked men and women my own age if they knew older people I might photograph and was surprised that many friends had someone special they wanted me to meet.

As my work progressed, I became much more optimistic about my own old age. The women spoke of advantages and privileges they found in these years. My new relationships with older women have affected me on many levels, including my dream life. For years I've had the troubling, recurrent dream of having to go back to college, only to find that there's no space for me in the dormitory. In a recent dream, though, I discovered an old building on the edge of campus with a Rooms for Rent sign in front. When I entered and took the elevator to the top, I was shown into a large, glassed-in game room. To my great surprise there were twenty old women hand-wrestling and tumbling about on the floor. They were having a marvelous time and invited me to join in.

It goes without saying that not all of us will gain admission to that room, but perhaps our chances can be increased if we free ourselves from stereotypical thinking and actually get to know older people we admire.

Pamela Valois, 1985

Postscript

Following the publication of *Gifts of Age* in 1985, the book took on a life of its own. A woman wrote, for example, that she had discovered it in a tiny alpine store at the end of a three-day backpacking trip in the North Cascades wilderness. Often enough, reactions to the book have been startlingly familiar: People have written saying "Here's someone special to me who should be in your next book." This same need to know and share a gifted elder is what inspired me in the first place.

P.V., 1989

Measuring Our Days

(for Bruce Black)

My student says: "My mother told me
only yesterday
that she was here in San Francisco
On V-J Day and she was twenty-five,
my age now.
She said it was an awful day for her,
some love she lost.
Something opened up
that belonged to me, it being hers,
a legacy."

That's why we do it—keep our books of days
when their measure
must remain unknown to us.
We forget to tell our children
(or fear to tell) so many things
about ourselves, when we were twenty-five
or ninety.

King David called the days we measure
a handbreadth, all vanity. He could sing
but as his heirs, we know
he wasn't right in everything.

                                        Charlotte Painter

JANUARY

Jacomena Maybeck

Born March 19, 1901

1

2

3

4

5

6

7

JANUARY

Alice Fong Yu
Born March 2, 1905

8

9

10

11

12

13

14

15

16

17

18

19

20

21

A lice was into taboo-busting. She wasn't going to sit back and be the widow of a university professor who limited herself to activity suitable to her years and status. She had poured her last faculty tea. . . . All those things she hadn't done when Bill was alive she had begun to do now just because they were in her, the perfectly harmless things she had done as a young girl: sailing, swimming, whistling, tap-dancing. That fun-loving nature of her childhood hadn't died; she just hadn't turned it loose all those years. Now it was taking over. Let other people worry about brittle bones if they wanted to—that was their lookout. Or the impropriety of a woman who sticks her fingers between her teeth to hail a cab. Let them think her a zany eccentric if they liked. She was through neglecting the part of herself that wanted to play.

Alice Lindberg Snyder

Born May 27, 1909

JANUARY

22

23

24

25

26

27

28

JANUARY

29

30

31

FEBRUARY

1

2

3

4

5

6

7

A worker at the Older Women's League said: "People who hadn't even met Tish often called here with their troubles. Maybe it'd be a woman with cancer, and Tish would sit there and listen, and try to get her onto a positive track." Tish was well informed about cancer, an old enemy. She had beaten it down in her forties, but just as she was beginning to organize OWL, it recurred, reminding her of her sustaining motto: "Organize, don't agonize." Tish had no time for agony at all. She was determined to press forward with her work for the rights of older women.

Tish Sommers

Born September 8, 1914

FEBRUARY

Jane Hollister Wheelright
Born September 9, 1905

8

9

10

11

12

13

14

FEBRUARY

15

16

17

18

19

20

21

"I love this part of my life as much as the beginning . . . these are the 'yes' years, when there is so much we can do—see our friends, write letters, read old ones. I might even make a book of stories for the children."

FEBRUARY

22

23

24

25

26

27

28/29

She had worried about old age since she was a child, never having seen anybody age gracefully. At twenty-one she had decided that chess would keep her mind alert and had learned the game for her old age. She had also studied braille, though she had her doubts if she would remember it now. Determined never to dampen the spirits of anybody younger, she studies, travels, and works for a theater. Among her rich rewards was a trip with her grandson—white water rafting.

Anna Keyes Neilsen

Born February 26, 1903

MARCH

Lucille Elliott
Born July 11, 1893

1

2

3

4

5

6

7

Hadn't she always said to her patients that the process of analysis was ongoing? Such a simple insight, of the sort she'd helped hundreds of people to make. She herself had to go blind before she could see its truth in her own life. She had always known that every darkness was the other side of a certain light, that the nether world existed to complement the whole. One door closes and another opens.

MARCH

8

9

10

11

12

13

14

She had learned early how to let go, to prepare for death. Sickness had guided her to learn how to relax every muscle of her body, so that she could teach others to do the same.

   She could always find a small space for herself, could go up above the walkway with the pink hawthorn, where the ground was carpeted with sorrel, to a flat spot carved out of the hill. There she could sit and meditate below the redwoods and gaze at the sky. She could have the hour alone that she needed every day to find the transition.

Ursula Hodge Casper

Born December 13, 1907

Lidia Puente Fielschmidt
Born February 8, 1907

15

16

17

18

19

20

21

MARCH

22

23

24

25

26

27

28

29

30

31

T

onight she wanted to dance. She'd be the first to arrive at The Good Table and the last to leave. She'd dance all night in her graduation dress. Wasn't that what they wanted, her friends, to see her accept what they offered, acknowledgment of the enduring verities, that friendships extend throughout a life, that loyalties are true, that life is good and rich as long as we have it? She was proof of all of that, and they were her team now—she couldn't let them down. She gathered up her notes on the tiny speech she'd promised to make about the scholarship fund. She added an opening comment she knew would make them laugh: "This is the kind of thing that doesn't happen to most people until after they are dead."

Margaret Calder Hayes

Born February 1, 1896

APRIL

1

2

3

4

5

6

7

APRIL

8

9

10

11

12

13

14

"**I** shall die young, at whatever age the experience occurs."

Watching for light is her vocation. Light and life are one and the same thing. There would be no life without light; it is the beginning; it is the substance that makes things visible, that brings humanity to an awareness of what cannot be seen. It can enhance a thing and make it holy. She feels this in her life as in her work, a sense of reaching for harmony beyond the human experience through light itself.

Ruth Bernhard

Born October 14, 1905

APRIL

Josephine Enizan Araldo
Born January 31, 1897

15

16

17

18

19

20

21

APRIL

22

23

24

25

26

27

28

If her work is about "the good life," there is also an ideal of goodness that informs it, as well as a wealth of learning and experience that always touches the spirit. When asked why she writes about food and hunger, the subject of so many of her essays that first appeared in the *New Yorker*, she said, "There is a communion of more than our bodies when bread is broken and wine is drunk."

29

30

The elderly student lifted her flower arrangement from the cut-glass vase and wrapped it in the newspaper that had been spread out on the table for trimmings. Then in embarrassment she realized how carefully everyone else was taking their arrangements home in vases. The woman shook her head. "I may be too old to learn flower arranging, Mrs. Obata," she said.

"Oh no," said Haruko humorously. "Ikebana is older than you, *very* old. Buddha was supposed to have had ikebana on his throne. If you know flower arranging, you do not grow old, for it is eternal."

Haruko Obata

Born February 10, 1892

MAY

1

2

3

4

5

6

7

"If old people are lonely and say everyone has left them and no one comes to see them, I say let them go. You do not need to have other people. You have the earth, the sun, the sky, the grass. You have yourself, and you can heal your mind by talking to the earth. Watch the grass, and you will learn how it grows from the earth and will be in touch again with the spirit that guides us."

MAY

8

9

10

11

12

13

14

. . . She

remembered herself in the late thirties at her early college job. She'd taught there for four years, even built a house. But they didn't renew her contract. Nothing was ever said to her about why, but she knew it had something to do with her affectional preference. She had been devastated. Of course, she knew things had changed on that campus. The experience had no charge now, not even in memory. That was how things used to be. . . . In fact, she was grateful for the way things had gone. It had been so comfortable in that small elitist college she might have stayed there forever, might never have gone on to teach in Guam or in Australia. Might never have met the woman she had lived with for eighteen years before her death. So much of her life had come about because of that single ostracism, so many good things.

Monika Kehoe

Born September 11, 1909

MAY

15

16

17

18

19

20

21

22

23

24

25

26

27

28

She preferred long walks on her native Hawaiian shores, visiting with seagulls, but her one-hundred-pound, five-foot frame needed the aerobic effect so she and her son had gone to buy the barbells and exercycle. The salesman had addressed his pitch to her son, until finally she spoke up timidly: "These are for me." Now, why should he be so surprised. After two months, muscle showed in the tricep, and on the beach she noticed more strength in her legs.

Peggy Hickok Hodge

Born December 26, 1914

MAY

29

30

31

JUNE

1 113

2

3

4

5

6

7

Painting and cooking—we'll never live long enough to learn the half of it. A passionate interest in what you do is the secret of enjoying life, perhaps the secret of long life, whether it is helping old people or children or making cheese or growing earthworms!

JUNE

8

9

10

11

12

13

14

She told us a little about her trip this summer in France, traveling on a Eurail Pass with a backpack (at eighty) to visit some out-of-the-way chefs. She told one of them that he was paying too much for broccoli. Notebooks of what she'd learned on this trip as well as those she'd written other summers were piled floor to ceiling in a back room. . . . It wasn't just her positive attitude in the kitchen but in the whole of life. Even when she was in pain, as she had been much of the last year, she said such things as, "I am good at standing pain; I am good at standing everything."

Josephine Enizan Araldo

Born January 31, 1897

JUNE

15

16

17

18

19

20

21

JUNE

22

23

24

25

26

27

28

There are certain beautiful things in the world that need to be recorded before they go away. Everything is ephemeral; nothing is the same from one moment to the next, whether because of light or time or weather. One of her photographs came back to mind in her time of trouble: a goose caught after poking its head between fence slats, stuck, unable to see a way out. Silly goose, it only needed a little guidance from someone with a larger picture, then its neck would be free.

Eleanor Milder Lawrence

Born November 23, 1910

JUNE

29

30

JULY

Ursula Hodge Casper
Born December 13, 1907

1

2

3

4

5

6

7

JULY

8

9

10

11

12

13

14

Oone day Josepha said, "I won't let my children play with whitey, that trash."

I wanted to help her release her obsession. I asked, "Josepha, would you work with a white person?"

"Naw, not if I could help it."

"You get along all right with me, don't you?" It was true, the girl conceded. "But you're Hispanic."

I explained to her that in El Salvador I was considered white. The members of my family were the equivalent of those white professionals that Josepha was so scornful of. I knew she was doing a disfavor to her child, passing on the inheritance of hate.

Lidia Puente Fielschmidt

Born February 8, 1907

JULY

15

16

17

18

19

20

21

JULY

22

23

24

25

26

27

28

She doesn't like to think of herself as a starter of things, but then she mentions the powerful people in her life: daughter Joan, whom she joins in the Humanitas cause of peace and human rights; daughter Mimi Farina, founder of Bread and Roses, taking entertainment to shut-ins and elders; the late Rosemary Goodenough, who persuaded Soledad prison to let inmates build a playground for their children's visits, a playground where Joan volunteers; and Kay Boyle, with whom she writes letters on behalf of political prisoners for Amnesty International. It's clear that she's at the starting line.

Joan Bridge Baez

Born April 11, 1913

JULY

Monika Kehoe
Born September 11, 1909

29

30

31

AUGUST

Marie LeMarquand Lovejoy
Born May 8, 1901

1

2

3

4

5

6

7

"To do good by stealth—that was the ideal I had always tried to follow. . . .
It was up to me to do the task I was assigned. The first rule of obedience goes
at least as far back as the *Bhagavad-Gita*—teaching that the gift of under-
standing comes through unquestioning service."

AUGUST

8

9

10

11

12

13

14

At fifty-seven she had decided to get another degree, in speech therapy. There were so many people who needed help, whose speech wasn't just right. When her son, Joal, had needed help with his speech, she learned that she had a knack for helping with the right placement of the tongue. So she had started on a wonderful new career: working with children, young people who were stuck, getting their tongues and lips to move into the right groove. The work brought a lot of laughter with it, and love.

Alice Fong Yu

Born March 2, 1905

AUGUST

15

16

17

18

19

20

21

"Old age is ten years beyond your own chronological age."

She started the support group for older women because she saw a need for it. "Why waste a perfectly good life just sitting around wanting somebody to invite you to do something when you could get busy, do it yourself, and include some of your friends in it."

AUGUST

22

23

24

25

26

27

28

S he has found plenty to do with her life and her wealth. Volunteering—her preferred term for "philanthropy" with its connotations of patronage—has become her way of life. "I guess I am self-motivated. I went to *them* about giving the symphony hall to San Francisco; they didn't come to me. Other people—a lot of people—would do things like that if they knew how, and would enjoy giving. Some people don't seem to enjoy having their money. It was a great pleasure for me to give that, and it should be for anybody, because you see people enjoying the hall."

Louise M. Davies

Born May 23, 1900

AUGUST

Margaret Briggs Gardner
Born December 7, 1895

29

30

31

She loves plants. Like people, they depend on you, they are friends. If they become unhealthy, it is as if a friend is ill. She used to enjoy playing violin duets with her son, but now gardening has become her passion. If her hands can't move swiftly enough on the strings, they are strong enough to pull weeds and dig. She loves to see her garden flourish. Her own health depends on it.

SEPTEMBER

1

2

3

4

5

6

7

Funny thing about the creative impulse—from time to time she'd think, that's all over, I don't want to make anything anymore, it's dried up. Then she'd be wandering by a gallery, or she'd be caught by the shape of something, a rock or an animal, and the next thing she knew she was out in her pot shop fiddling around with the clay, letting the pieces come out. It was irrepressible, the desire to make things. She knew well enough not to worry when it went away, it always came back, like a welcome friend. One privilege about being old was that she didn't have to worry about competition; a few years back she had felt obligated to make things that would look good in an exhibition. Now she just made things that seemed to want to get made, like this horse whose glaze she was finishing: blue and white he was, and bristling with his own energy.

Jacomena Maybeck

Born March 19, 1901

SEPTEMBER

8

9

10

11

12

13 A very special lady was born today in 1910. We were lucky to have her.

14

SEPTEMBER

Cecil Pierce
Born October 22, 1908

15

16

17

18

19

20

21

Somehow a friend persuaded Cecil to go with her to an art class at a senior center. Cecil had never seen herself as a senior center type, but since her retirement, she had noticed a tendency in herself to experiment. And now, thinking in "types" is an act of the enemy.

SEPTEMBER

22

23

24

25

26

27

28

On her seventy-fifth birth-day, her daughter's house was completely cleared of furniture, tables laid with pink cloths. Her sister even flew in from Denver. And little David gave a skit in which he played a sheik who whispered in her ear, "Come with me to the Casbah," mixing up movies he probably never saw, except in TV clips. They had put together a whole slide show of her family from baby pictures through to that picnic last summer, in a take-off on "This is Your Life."

Virginia Walsh

Born December 29, 1907

SEPTEMBER

29

30

"I have one more adaptation I must make in life, then I'll be through. I want to adapt to the idea of death. It's important that I shouldn't be afraid of death. I'm not as much afraid now as twenty years ago, but I still have work to do. There's a certain laziness that I'm anxious to overcome. I should just go about it calmly and get on better terms with death. I hope I can adapt to it as well as I have to everything else."

OCTOBER

1

2

3

4

5

6

7

The conference had received her paper well. "The Power of the Maiden." They understood her: Let the maiden archetype in ourselves give us access to all female experience, that of both future and past as felt through daughter, wife, mother, worker, wise woman. The Navajos had always known of these capacities, acknowledged them in their "changing-woman goddess," while our modern world stumbled along with two roles, "young girl" and "old girl." Wasn't it the maiden in a woman's psyche, for example, who prompted a woman with children to go back to college or to take a plunge into some new adventure?

Jane Hollister Wheelright

Born September 9, 1905

OCTOBER

8

9

10

11

12

13

14

OCTOBER

Anna Keyes Neilsen
Born February 26, 1903

15

16

17

18

19

20

21

OCTOBER

22

23

24

25

26

27

28

In her bindery room, she takes out her new project. She is grateful for this late-life career. To make something last or come back to life, something rare and beautiful—that is worth any amount of trouble. To learn book-binding she had traveled all over—Japan, England, Italy. She hadn't always been timid about traveling. But just now she had said no when her nephew Maurice invited her to go to Japan with him. She was touched that he thought of traveling with her, but she was eighty-six! She'd be too much trouble. *To make something last*, she muses. She reaches for the phone. She says, "Maurice, it sounds too good to miss. I'll go with you."

Stella Nicole Patri

Born November 1, 1896

OCTOBER

29

30

31

NOVEMBER

1

2

3

4

5

6

7

Frances had begun thinking about senior citizen's centers a long time ago. There wasn't any concern about the aged in her grandmother's day. She went to the community board and discovered that many people were undernourished because they lived alone and never got out, so she got busy doing something about it. . . . The centers stood for an idea whose time had come. People were beginning to understand that if they lived, they too, would be old someday.

Frances Mary Albrier

Born September 21, 1898

NOVEMBER

Joan Bridge Baez
Born April 11, 1913

8

9

10

11

12

13

14

NOVEMBER

Tish Sommers
Born September 8, 1914

15

16

17

18

19

20

21

NOVEMBER

22

23

24

25

26

27

28

"**M**y church has formed the Inez Marks Club to support my schools in China. My daughter, Wester, saw the schools only last year. . . . She found that the first kindergarten in all of western China, which I opened, was still there. Of course, the revolution had taken them over and changed everything, all of China. I used to say it'd take a century to do away with footbinding, but it was done away with in a year or two. . . . People could do that with the bomb if they wanted. You can do away with any evil. It's a matter of believing it is possible to stop making bombs. Like footbinding, we could just stop doing it."

Inez Marks Lowdermilk

Born January 26, 1890

NOVEMBER

29

30

When asked why she bothered to study the family tree, Ethel used to quote her young cousin: "Because I want to know why I feel the way I do about Beethoven, spinach, and companionate marriage."

DECEMBER

Florence Niles Jury
Born August 24, 1906

1

2

3

4

5

6

7

Having young people in my life is . . . very important. This seems perfectly natural to me, but I think young people are often afraid of older people. Perhaps it's the judgmental part. Elders sometimes give off an aura of being critical. Some of this must be because they don't *know* young people. For myself, I'm interested in hearing a different viewpoint than my own because in a way, I'm terribly conservative.

DECEMBER

8

9

10

11

12

13

14

H

er nature is movement.

She used to say, "I ran fast and never looked back."

The dance is an ephemeral art, movement in time and space, then over so quickly. . . . The dances she learned from Ruth St. Denis must be preserved, and Klarna has the commitment she misses in the young. She is the keeper of the flame.

Klarna Pinska

Born January 7, 1902

DECEMBER

Peggy Hickok Hodge
Born December 26, 1914

15

16

17

18

19

20

21

DECEMBER

Ruth Pennell
Born February 23, 1903

22

23

24

25

26

27

28

Shelley has become her companion in age. She'd adopted him from a give-
away box at Wells Fargo Bank seventeen years ago. Always her own woman,
telling the United Nations Story on her radio series, building a house by herself
in the Trinity Alps, she could manage well as a widow with her two sons gone.
But how good to have Shelley's dependable responses and unqualified devo-
tion. A friend she could always count on to be there for her. You can't rule out
the need everyone alive has for touching, either.

DECEMBER

29

30

31

For nearly six decades the bells in the Campanile at the University of California, Berkeley campus, were rung by a delicate, slender woman whose bright red hair slowly turned silvery white as she became what she called "part of the public domain."

She went through a bit of conflict with the math professors, who wanted her to ring only traditional changes. But why not learn the *meaning* of the word change, see its connection to life? You had to go with what was coming next, even if it was *tunes* on the chimes or the whole enormous carillon of bells they had now. You had to allow things to move along, or give up your nostalgia. Nothing remained the same, not even the ringing of changes.

Margaret Murdock

Born June 22, 1894

Died June 10, 1985